rosemary

© Copyright 2021 Hanna Dunbar-Bruce

written during the worst year of my life
dedicated to
micheal george-bruce and rosemary ann dunbar
my father and grandmother

POEM LIST

INTRODUCTION

ROSEMARY ANN

LETTER TO HEAVEN

WHAT IS WORSE THAN DEATH?

DISORDERED

A DOCTOR AND HIS PATIENT

BIG BLUE EYES

ATTACK

THE WORLD SPIN

ACTIONS SPEAK LOUDER THAN WORDS

LUNGS

RAINY DAY

CELESTIAL MOVEMENT

UNTIL MY FATHER DIED

THE EARLY BIRD CATCHES THE SANDWICH

SPACE

OBESITY

A MESSAGE FOR THE STARS

BODY DYSMORPHIA

A ROSEMARY IS A ROSEMARY IS A ROSEMARY

RAIN AND DUST

BACK TO THE BLUESIDE

NO ONE COULD CARE AS MUCH AS ME

SOMETIMES IS MORE THAN OFTEN

GRIM REAPER

FEEL

SKYFALL

PILLS AND SHOES

A MESSAGE FOR THE STARS 2.0

FALLING APART

GARDEN SEGREGATION

BON- APPETIT

DREAM CATCHER

FINAL GOODBYES

SONGS OF EXPERIENCE / WILLIAM BLAKE

4:00AM LATE NIGHT CONVERSATIONS

500 CALORIES A DAY KEEPS THE INSECURITIES AWAY

LETTER TO MY PAST SELF

WILLOW WISPS

ETERNITY

SHE WAS THE FOREST HE WAS THE FIRE

A TRAIN RIDE

FLY AWAY CAGED BIRD

SOCIAL ANXIETY AT ITS FINEST

INSOMNIA

SYSTEM ERROR

ROBERT FROST

POST-SECONDARY

SATURATION

PHOENIX

DRAGON

FAIRY TALE

UNTIL YOU CANNOT ANYMORE

A SMALL POCKET

GHOST

BLUE WHALE

THEY NEVER TOLD LIFE IT WAS GONNA BE THIS WAY

END GAME

ROAD TRIPS

SELFISH

GOODNIGHT

A PERSON I KNEW

3:55am

HOW I HANDLE DEATH

DEATH AND HIS WINE / A SHORT STORY

GOODBYE

WHAT I'VE LEARNED

DEAR ROSEMARY

INTRODUCTION / THE WORST YEAR OF MY LIFE

it's so easy to exaggerate the phrase "the worst blah blah of my life". if you're late for work, lose your wallet, and lock your keys in the car all in the same day, you may tweet out "i just had the worst day of my life ." but tomorrow your keys will still be there, you'll be on time and by next week your new ID's will already be shipped out by whatever government official place does so for you.

but when i say this compilation of poetry was written in the worst year of my life, i don't mean it as a cliche or hyperbole to exaggerate losing my car keys or having an immense amount of social drama. the year in which these poems are of context was a year i lost more than any person should ever have to fathom within such a short timeframe. i went from being a naive child just trying to find what i wanted to do with the rest of my life, battling love and romance, to facing the fact that pieces of my childhood, souls i had known my whole life were just slipping away from me like fluffy dandelions seed-wisps in early june.

it started with my grandmother, my mother's mother, a comical, beautiful, supportive, full of love and energetic woman who could make you smile no matter what mood you were in. she was diagnosed with pulmonary fibrosis, a disease of the lungs. i sat by her hospital bed with my family, every minute, of every day, for one week straight, while she lay unconscious waiting to die. my grandfather laid on a chair at her feet and stared at her, savouring the last moments of his soulmate. her final words to me were "you're going to be ok" and she said this as she held my cheek.

but mimi, you were so wrong, because your death was a beginning to a string of many more unfortunate events.

then my dog, then my bunny. they died too. why did they die? i still don't know. i convinced myself death comes in sets of three, but that year death felt like an infinity. but i put a smile on my face and every morning served my trauma sunny side up and swallowed it.

if no one knew i was sad, then maybe i would just one day wake up and not be sad.

it worked for a while- pushing it down.
pretending it didn't exist.

until july hit.

and this is where the child inside of me died.

in july my father was diagnosed with cancer. every day i would visit him in the hospital, for a week straight as he proceeded to get tests done. i'd sit by his side like a shadow, as he cried, as he laughed, as he slept. i watched him as he looked out the window and said "hanna i'm not ready to die. i look outside and think is this the last time i'll ever see this?". what do you say to that? i simply sighed and said, "daddy you're not going to die."

daddy … i'm sorry i lied.

because he did die. when we found out he was stage three lung cancer and had only a few months to live he died the next night.
he died the next night.
he died the next night.
i remember him in the emergency room, attached to machines, clinging onto my hand, eyes bulging out of his head, and i couldn't help but cry. he was terrified to die and i was terrified of him dying. when they pronounced him dead i remember screaming, and the rest was a blur. his last words were to me, who sat at the foot of his bed, laying my head in my hand. he said, even though he was at the brink of death, "hanna, are you sleepy?".
 yes daddy, i am sleepy.
i am so sleepy.
im so sleepy because this world is so tiring.

but the world keeps turning,
you know, the world keeps turning.
 and now i count the dead.
     i count the dead, i say their names because if i don't forget their names, wherever they are, i pray they won't forget mine.

ROSEMARY ANN

rosemary ann
rosemary can
rosemary can you
rosemary can you tell
rosemary can you tell me
rosemary can you tell me why
rosemary can you tell me why the
rosemary can you tell me why the world
rosemary can you tell me why the world is
rosemary can you tell me why the world is so
rosemary can you tell me why the world is so sad

LETTER TO HEAVEN

dear rosemary,

as i get older i find that the
world is getting so much colder.
things that seem so simple
to everyone else
seem so complex to myself.
i feel like i should be smarter,
i'm wise,
but everyone else seems wiser.
i'm a step behind everyone around me,
and fifty steps behind who i want to be.
i promised you i would be something great,
that i'd heal my heart that's full of hate.
you told me that i would be ok,
and i try so hard to do what you say.
i try not to think of you and cry,
i try not to think of daddy and how fast he died.
i try not to look at my family and want to say
goodbye.
i try and i try and i try and i try and i try
and i try and i try and i ———

dear rosemary,
as i get older, i find that the
the world is getting so much colder.

WHAT IS WORSE THAN DEATH?

i always think there's something worse than death,
with the way people scream and cry.
don't get me wrong,
i also screamed and cried when my father died,
but still i always think there's something worse than death.
 i feel like i'm sitting and waiting
for the devil to reach his hand up
from the depths of hell and drag me, the dying
back down with him,
handprint burned into thighs,
the heat evaporating tears that fell
from that final cry.
i'm waiting for the monster,
whose teeth are more terrifying than not breathing,
to rip pieces of flesh off one by one,
throwing their head back in sadistic pleasure
and swallowing screams with laughter,
because the worst thing that can happen to you
doesn't come after your journey on the river of styx,
but there must be something else,
something more terrifying.

i always think there's something worse than death.
i don't know what's wrong with me.
i really just don't seem to find death that scary.
it's always the worst-case scenario
yet i feel there are a million things i'd fear more
then closing my eyes forever.
i fear living.
i fear pain.
i fear the sorrow i'll face
when i lose someone i love again.
i fear the future but also the past.
i fear living in the present,
i fear saying goodbye
 and i fear finishing last.

i fear the shadows that creep around my room at night,
leaning over my face and punching a hole into my chest.
i fear telling people how i feel,
i fear letting them down.
i fear the sharks that swim around me when i'm trapped in my head.
i fear spiders and i fear heights,
i don't trust people who get high on life.
i'm terrified of God and what he'd say to me
if i opened my ears and tried to listen.
i'm scared of people who rely on me,
their eyes wide and glisten
with freshly coated tears waiting for me to say
some poetic words to take their pain away.
i fear going blind and losing my mind,
i fear one day people will realize
i'm not a good enough reason for them to stay.
i fear black cats that cross me by late at night,
because with the life i've lived i can't afford any more bad luck
and then i fear my mind because how could i
look at an innocent creature and only see evil.
i fear looking in the mirror because i hate what i see.
i fear my stomach, my thighs, my hair and my body.
i fear my reflection that looks back at me,
i fear it's smile and i think it's ugly.
i fear the words it whispers in my head,
when it tells me that i'd be better off dead-
but i don't think being dead is the worst thing that can happen to me.
i do not fear death.
at some point in this life, i must have started looking at death
and seeing it as a blessing.
a gift we get when we finish life,
 because what living has taught me is
there are a lot of things worse than death.

DISORDERED

"in-between"
my therapist said,
with a smile on his face
after i asked
if i was insane.
that i was

in-between.

not happy, not manic
just,

in-between.

i'm not disordered
but i'm not
    i n
or de r.

i'm a solidified fragment
falling from the sky of sanity
trapped on a branch
of an old tree,
waiting to fall
waiting for fly
waiting to die.

A DOCTOR AND HIS PATIENT

there was a doctor who asked their patient why they wanted to die.
the patient smiled, let out a giggle and looked that doctor in the eye.
then with a smirk on their pale and exhausted face,
said "tell me, doctor, exactly why do you work in this place?

are you a doctor because you want to save the lives of everyone?
or are you a doctor because you're simply just dumb?"
the doctor was shocked at the patient's question,
and had to think about it closely- to find the lesson.

"i do not think i understand what you mean,"
the doctor said, shaking his head at a comment so obscene.
the patient smiled again, and this time replied
"do you not realize that to help all these people you set your life aside,

you let your youth melt off your fingers
studying textbooks and analyzing figures,
you do CPR when someone is about to die,
when really, it's pointless, because we all will die sometime?

what do doctors really do, i have to stop and wonder,
then simply give some medicine and a couple more years to suffer."
the doctor let his mouth fall open,
because he knew it was true, what the patient had spoken,

it didn't make it right, but it certainly wasn't wrong,
the doctor was just giving the inevitable a chance to prolong.
"even if we're all going to die,
with this fact i think we both see eye to eye,

what about the moments in between?
the things we wake up in the morning to see,
those are the things that make life worth living,
those are the moments that by saving lives we are giving."

the patient shook their head, because they couldn't help but disagree,
there are no moments, no rising sun or other reason to make them believe
that any part of this miserable and painful life was worth living.
the patient did not think living was the same as just existing.

BIG BLUE EYES

they used to tell me
that i had eyes that sparkled.
they'd gleam and they glowed
even when i heaved and hoed.
i could pull trees from the ground
by their roots with my hands
but they'd still look at me
and say my eyes sparkled like
pearls in the sand.

but now my eyes are dull and boring,
from all the time i stayed up
till morning
all the nights
i weeped and woed.
my arms are too weak for trees,
and eyes to swollen to sparkle,
too lost in a constant state
of warning and mourning.

ATTACK
i'm under attack by my own mind.

how fucked up.

THE WORLD SPIN

do you sometimes feel the world spin?
when you lay in your bed,
on the brink of dreaming
late at night?

or perhaps early in the morning.
when your mind is alive
 but your body is asleep.

sometimes i can feel gravity pulling me
like water rolling off a cliff,
i feel a faded part of my soul ripped away
and drift to the edges of my skin.

i feel myself being dragged away.

sometimes i can feel the world spin
if i close my eyes at the right moment.

sometimes i can feel the world spin.

ACTIONS SPEAK LOUDER THAN WORDS

the reason words
hurt so much
is because words are thoughts
and thoughts become beliefs
and beliefs become actions
and actions
well,
 actions speak louder than words

LUNGS

rosemary,

can you believe the creator took my father too?
made me hear the death rattle from his chest
just like i did with you?
we whispered "i love you"
and gave terrifying hugs,
then the lord his soul would take
from the air inside his lungs.

jesus,
rosemary,
why is it always the lungs?

RAINY DAY

even clouds
even clouds
turn grey and cry...

CELESTIAL MOVEMENT

i'm like an ocean
calm on the surface
but a shark pit underneath.

it's only when the moon rises
and moves my tides
my exterior starts to stir.

UNTIL MY FATHER DIED

every time i go to sleep
i see my father die.
the endorphins in my brain like to get creative.
sometimes he dies in a bed,
sometimes he dies in my arms.
other times he's on the clouds,
already dead and asking me why
i'm there with him.

one time i had a dream i called him on the phone,
screaming with all my might, "daddy why did you leave me alone?"
i didn't understand he was on the other line,
until he told me that everything was fine.
but in the dream when i went to his side,
he was still full of cancer, eating him alive.
so, in my dream i got on my knees and cried,
"please God can he just stay alive this time?"

then when i woke up, i felt the urge to call him.
but the realization washed over me that i would never reach him,
and once again i felt the familiar empty sting-
i never knew emptiness could even sting
until my father died.
i never knew how monsters could grab your thighs,
pull you close and eat a hole into your stomach,
feasting on the nothing within.
consuming empty calories, feeding off my skin.
condemning me like i was a sin.

i never knew that happiness could be drained like water in a bath.
i never knew how long i could hold my breath
as i stood in the chaos of the aftermath,
memories on fire burning in pieces stinging my face,
i need to find a way to get out of this place.

but i never felt the need to run and hide
until the day my father died.

THE EARLY BIRD CATCHES THE SANDWICH

the noise my pillow made
when i moved my head
reminded me of the sleepless
nights i spent at my grandparents' house
as a kid.

tossing and turning, undiagnosed insomnia
keeping me awake all night,
until the clock hit 5am,
and my two small feet hit the floor
shuffling quietly across the hall
to my grandparents' room,
quietly and carefully to not wake up
my sleeping grandfather, grouchy as he can be.

i shuffle my way to my mimi's side of the bed
and breathe in her smell.
quietly i whisper for her to wake up
and she jumps up with a "huh"
then throws her feet over the side,
putting on her slippers and
grabbing her robe, the same robe as always.

we make our way to the kitchen
where she makes me a cheese sandwich
on a blue and white plate.
then we go downstairs to the basement living room.
she puts on morning cartoons for me,
while she curls up on the couch,
 legs tucked behind her,
to sleep a couple more hours.

i'd give anything, anything i possibly could
to relive a morning like this,
that all started with the rustling of a pillow.

SPACE

my voice always seems so small in this world
where billions on billions of sounds
are so loud they fill   space   .

OBESITY

i take up too much space.
i take up too much space so i
pull my shoulders in and press
my thighs tightly together.
i inhale my stomach and keep my head down,
i do not look anyone in the eye.
when i do i think "i take up too much space,"
and then i retreat into my head
where my monsters whisper all the things
everyone around me leaves unsaid,
"she takes up too much space.
she has an ugly face.
it's such a disgrace,
if i were her, i'd leave this place,"
my eyes leak with hate from my brain
but it's not my thoughts the monsters say,
no, it's the thoughts of those around me who
don't take up too much space.
they read their thoughts aloud like an open book
and i keep my head down afraid to look
around at the people who look at me because
we both know
i
take up too much space.

A MESSAGE FOR THE STARS

i can't understand, rosemary
i can't understand
how particles and atoms
form into catastrophe.

and if stars can live a million years
why couldn't they share some time with you?

BODY DYSMORPHIA

we do these things to our bodies
because our bodies do these things to our minds
and it's so fucking toxic
but we do it all the fucking time

A ROSEMARY IS A ROSEMARY IS A ROSEMARY

a rose is a rose is a rose is a rose
a rose by any name
wouldn't be as beautiful
as a rosemary.

RAIN AND DUST

the saddest tears
are the hot heavy ones
that roll down your cheeks
like raindrops on a glass window.

so heavy you start to crack
then shatter until your spirit
is nothing but irrelevant dust,
sifting across cement in a graveyard.

BACK TO THE BLUESIDE

i feel myself slipping
into the deepest parts
of the oceans
that i
tried so hard to escape,
and i can feel the salt
fill up my lungs
and stain them,
water coloured blue
        water coloured blue

NO ONE COULD CARE AS MUCH AS ME

i always say
"i don't give a shit"
"i don't give a fuck"
but i care too much
and that's my fucking problem.

SOMETIMES IS MORE OFTEN THAN OFTEN

sometimes i
hold my fingers to my nose
and feel my breath.

sometimes i
put my fingers against my wrist
and feel my pulse.

sometimes i
do all of this to feel
the life inside of me.

because

sometimes i
feel that it would be
better to be dead.

GRIM REAPER

you never think of death
until your bones ache
and your hands ripple
with every move.

but death could be anywhere.
he could be   m i l e s   away,
around the corner,
or sleeping in your bed.

FEEL

do i miss you?
or do i miss the way you
made me feel?
could make me feel?
had made me feel?
just make me feel…
i just want to feel
           again.

SKYFALL

lately, the sky is full of stars,
each night just a little closer.

perhaps they're falling for you too.

PILLS AND SHOES

medication is like a pair of shoes.
they start off new and great,
but overtime wear down
and aren't effective anymore.

i wonder if it's better to just be barefoot.

A MESSAGE FOR THE STARS 2.0

once again, i look at the stars.
and the stars are so selfish,
they live a million years
and still come out at night
to watch us die.

so i hate the stars,
because they couldn't share eternity
with my dearest grandmother,
a vibrant rose who died in this dusty world.

FALLING APART

falling apart is like when the water in the shower starts to turn cold. you can feel the change, but there's nothing you can do. once the warmth is gone
                                                        it's gone.

the water keeps running
    but it's cold as ice.

GARDEN SEGREGATION

if we treated dandelions like roses
maybe the world wouldn't be so
                                        unjust.

BON-APPETIT -

betrayal is a meal i eat.
plated nicely with the finest silver.
sliced nicely into small pieces
easier to devour.

and then you devour me.

whatever remains,
after you are full,
you take a sledgehammer
and shatter me into pieces,
then ask why i have trust issues.

a person can only handle so much heartbr e a k.

DREAM CATCHER

weaved by wrinkled hands. collecting dust, time stands still. overcome with slumber, slumping onto a cloud of clear and concise vivid, parallel motion please, lines of wonderland webbed in the wires. fear fathom reach here in the world circled with industrial netted diamonds. died a thousand times and a thousand more. one cannot say, one cannot know, one has not threaded needles three times through then pull and cut please. one has not experienced, you, me, us, we, i, one must learn what's lost in webbed wires of circular hopes cast by chance into dreams where yellow moon gardens cast shadows across spilt milk in which is not yet soured, but surely past expiration.
    Let us dream, catching spirit.
        catch my spirit fallen between
            the threads in wonderland

FINAL GOODBYES

i held you close to my chest
and whispered goodnight,
but you were never there
for good morning.

SONGS OF EXPERIENCE / WILLIAM BLAKE

oh father oh father
where art thou gone?
do you ride on the clouds
and the sun with
the morning dawn?

4:00AM LATE NIGHT CONVERSATIONS

message sent

do you ever think that like the people who die that we love miss us as much as we miss them, but it just doesn't hurt them because they understand and know the secrets of life and death and like we don't, so they know they'll see us again and even though they miss us also it's just a waiting game for them, but for us we never ever ever know if we'll see them again so it's very hard and painful and they're just up there like "don't worry, in a few years we'll be together again, it'll go by faster than you think" because like i really really hope that's how it is.

500 CALORIES A DAY KEEPS THE INSECURITIES AWAY

skinny
s k i n n y
skinny
s
k
i
n
n
y
i won't stop until my bones
can be grated through my skin
on stones.

LETTER TO MY PAST SELF

never fall for a boy
whose eyes are blue.

he'll invite you over for breakfast
and then break your heart by noon.

but in the end if you do
don't forget, i tried to warn you.

WILLOW-WISPS

loving you is like following willow-wisps into a forest at night. i'm captivated by your celestial light. i'm so blinded by your beauty i can't see the monstrosity hidden underneath it. i could never seek you out in day, but my god at night you shone

                                                          so bright.
i felt like the first moth attracted to electricity. amazed. dazzled.

i will never comprehend how your light turned out to be a trap. my wings i had just started to spread were ripped off at the seams of my spine, leaving fragments of bones

                                              on the floor
                                   with my fallen wing dust.
but its my fault.
because within all the poems i read, all the celtic folklore i swallowed in stories, i should have known that willow-wisps aren't meant to be caught.

                but oh boy they love to taunt.

and honestly i'd rather be trapped on a mountain or lost at sea
then lost in a forest following a boy who was supposed to love me.

willow-wisps love to be followed
and love to be loved

but they don't love to love.

ETERNITY

just pain
just pain
just pain
just pain
just pain
it's always
just pain

SHE WAS THE FOREST HE WAS THE FIRE

she with mad intensity
picked her garden off his spine
that she too long watered with tears.
and he in calm sinister
traced the left-over weeds
remembered how the garden butterflies
use to flutter their wings upon his lips.

she remembered the thunderstorms of his heart
as her veins grew over his chest
wrapping him in their natural grasp.
she who sat up preening herself in the moonlight.
he who dragged his fingers along her back
drizzling seeds inside of her.

the garden he planted was full of thorns
and lasted through every season,
but hers died when the weather grew cold
and all that's left in him is a barren memory
and a pile of dirt
where her love used to create photosynthesis.

A TRAIN RIDE

autumn raindrops roll down the window
unbothered by the slicing wind of faith.
three drops like thread
leaving trails of aquatic clouds
as they disappear to the tracks.

i think my string has been cut
for i am emotionally detached
in case you did not know.

three women sit
dripping drops down from their fingertips.
their cruel gaze and piercing eyes
solidify the cloud tears
and make them physically fit
for the journey they take
down the windowpane

and as we go, faster faster, into the country
the drops are thrown off the train
with no emotion.
was it man who killed these raindrops?
or did they throw themselves onto the ground
because the train was simply going too fast

even the fates cry.

FLY AWAY CAGED BIRD

nightingales fly around you.
doves and
blue jays, even robins.
but i am caught in the claws of
hawks and crows.
a murder, a murder
they murder they murder
a death is a death is a death is a death

sing sweet nightingale
i hear you from my windowsill.

SOCIAL ANXIETY AT ITS FINEST

people annoy me.
maybe it's their oversized foreheads
or their wicked crescent moon smiles.
maybe it's the expectations i didn't want,
and demands i'm obligated to meet.

people really really annoy me.
their faces bug me.
it starts in my stomach and burns my whole body.
i want to puke.
i want to scream,
"don't look at me!".

people really fucking annoy me,
but only because they fill me with anxiety.

INSOMNIA

nighttime sonatas
are the saddest of them all.
where moon birthed fairies
cast moon cursed spells
tossing and turning
all night.

my thoughts are louder than
the nocturnal music.
sweet melodies of hope
that this may be
my final hours
sing me to sleep,

mornings are a disappointment,
and a lifetime necessity.

SYSTEM ERROR

the person in which danced in pastoral
is dead.
all that's left is an empty shell and its controller,
in a system called me.
CTRL smile.
CTRL laugh.

system error.
system error.

ROBERT FROST

some people burn in fire
a humid flame lit by desire,
and those people i can't help but admire.

they must be so warm.

but for me i'm sheeted with black ice.
crafted by water, perfectly precise.
surely to freeze to death would also suffice.

i am so cold.

POST-SECONDARY

i'm wasting my prime on books and stories
analyzing poetry from the 1940's
lines of woe
and lines or ho-
riffic scenes of heaven and hell
reading tales from when lucifer fell
as my prime sifts through an hourglass full of sand
trapped inside my educational wasteland.

SATURATION

you need to learn to love yourself at least one percent more than you hate yourself.
that one percent is enough to take a black and white world,
and give it a tint of colour.

PHOENIX

have you ever stood in the ashes
 of the person you used to be?
embers still dimly glowing
and burning the last fragments of yourself,
while you stand and watch
memories play in the smoke
and d   r   i   f   t away,
blending into clouds?

i have.

DRAGON

what is a fireless dragon,
if not just a serpent in the grass
hiding from the eyes of hawks?

FAIRYTALE

i wanted to write a poem here,
about kings and queens and knights.

i wanted to write a poem here,
with visions and beautiful sights!

but honestly,
i was too depressed.

UNTIL YOU CANNOT ANYMORE

we all just keep living
until we cannot live
anymore.
whether that be physically,
or in some cases
emotionally.

A SMALL POCKET

when i'm gone
by all means
put me in a small pocket
at the back of your mind,
but please
just don't let me
      go

GHOST

i do not know
if i love you
or the ghost
that took host
of the person
you used to be

BLUE WHALE

i find it hard to breathe
because my lungs are bruised
black and blue
from all the whales
that swim in and out
like sewing needles on fabric
through my rib cage.
they found me at the bottom
of the ocean i flooded,
just a carcass of a ship
that once sailed through the seas
instead of being swallowed by them.

THEY NEVER TOLD LIFE IT WAS GONNA BE THIS WAY

why do i make jokes about my depression?
why do i treat it like a personality trait, like an obsession?
how do i take my trauma, the weight on my lungs
that people try too hard to keep hidden
deep in holes that they dug
in the back of their minds as if speaking these thoughts are forbidden?

a dark plum on a tree in the garden of Eden,
planted but never picked,
because it's much better to eat apples and peaches
then dark plums of corruption
but where did they get adam and eve?
the apples were just as poisoning,
as the dark plumb in that tree.

no, i won't let myself be poisoned by any fruit.
i will not choke on the seeds of happy apples,
and i will not vomit juices of plums then kneel in front of a chapel,
begging God to take my pain away.
i look my pain in the face,
i stare at it eye to eye and i say
"you will not win even if i die,
because if you want to kill me,
then i will take you down with me.
one sick, twisted, messed up joke at a time."

and at the end when i question my worth,
when i look back at my body
and see my soul has left this earth,
i will look life in the eyes,
that became pale when my time came to a halt
and ask "what was this all for?"

but i have a feeling life's answer will be,
"there is no meaning to why we suffer,
it was humans who took me away,
hid me in the shadows.
they favoured existing over living,
and as much as i tried to scream and shout,

you silly humans told me to shut my mouth,
because if you are living you cannot be oppressed.
if you are living you cannot be suppressed.
if you are living you will not be depressed.
when you're existing you are not much of a threat."

i know life will say those words,
and my depression will smile.
then it'll begin to melt and turn to juice,
sipped in the glass of another innocent child.

we are all cursed.

END GAME

i just want someone who would risk it all
the way i would for them...
someone who will always be there
and not leave when things get rough
someone who will wipe my tears away
and tell me it's ok when things are tough
someone who can take all my broken pieces
and glue them back together with love

does that person exist?

ROAD TRIPS

two clouds
seconds away from cracking open
held each other in their arms
and dissolved into one another
until their lips met
and they shared their first kiss
then evaporated into rain

SELFISH

i've let you push me off mountains
just to see me fly.
tie anchors to my ankles
just to see my sink.
i've sifted through hour glasses
and turned to bubbles in sand,
just to stay near you.

but you're so selfish
cause you'd never do the same.

GOODNIGHT

darkness creeps
when night is deep
and seeps into my mind.

one two three
the rest of me
isn't far behind.

A PERSON I KNEW

if you have a moment let me tell you about a person i once knew.
this person was beautiful.
in all the cliches i could possibly use
this person was beautiful.
when you looked into their eyes
the stars would get jealous because they knew
they could never compete with the beauty of those eyes.

when this person smiled
they threw their whole heart into that smile
without hesitation.
they wore emotion like a new knit sweater,
and let you feel the soft sleeves of it.
you could not not fall in love with this person.
and when you fell,
as you inevitably will
they'd hold your hand and fall with you.

but sometimes the seams of the sweater would begin to pull,
and the edges of the smile would begin to crack.
you would look at this person
who threw their head back and laughed
as they fell in love alongside you
and only see a ghost-
a carcass of who they used to be.

they wore their emotions like a sweater
and they wore their sadness like a shackle.
a weighted anchor trapping you and them at the bottom of an ocean
because you fell in love so hard
you're glued to that hand until the very end.

now the eyes that sparkled are shot down by angry stars
who waited in the shadows to seek revenge
on the beauty that took the attention away from them-
leaving that beautiful person blind.
they cannot see all the people who are in love with them
gripping onto their hand,
tying themselves to anchors.

that person throws their head back and laughs
as they sink deeper and deeper,
and they sigh when the anchor stabs their stomach
and pins them to the bottom of the ocean.
saltwater blood stains my cheeks red
but i would not have it any other way,
because if this person is dead then me too.
me too.
me too.

i was only falling in love,
but they were falling apart.
isn't that funny?

3:55am

i like to sit in my sadness. i let it wash over me in an uncomfortable wave, filling up all the holes the world has pierced in me. i let the sting of saltwater depression wash out my wounds and remind me that i feel like this because i am too alive. my jaw is not tight, and my air is not gone- i am comfortable because i am numb. i am used to the feeling of a hole in my stomach and i know not to move because if i do it will rip open and everything will come spilling out. i stay still as anxiety urchins crawl over my legs, my arms and stab my brain as if they were going to perform a lobotomy to make me ok. i stay still because if i move and let it all spill out sharks will become attracted to the scent of my weakness or take advantage of my pain and i will not be taken advantage of and i will not become the prey. when the worst is over, i swim over to a cage and lock myself into it. the urchins still cling onto my body but i ignore them and carry on with my day. my wounds still sting, and my lungs are sore. my skin is disintegrating off my face and even when i "feel ok" i am still falling apart. small fish swim by and take pieces of me with them. i just let them go. take all the pieces you need. let me feed you, let my brokenness be your uplifting, be your survival. i am only the worth of my pain.

HOW I HANDLE DEATH

everyone is always so shocked with how well i handle death.
i make jokes about cancer,
i make jokes about loss.
people may get uncomfortable,
but my jokes always come with a cost.
i bounce back right away,
living my life like it never happened.
i push it all to the side,
and lock it deep in my memory.
and everyone says, "how do you handle death?"
and they come to me for advice.
so, i stick up my head, and begin my string of lies.

because the truth is i am traumatized.
it feels like those who have been gone only died days ago.
i refuse to accept the fact my dad is dead and let him go.
i never let anyone around me know,
that when my grandmother died, i threw my arms around her body
and wanted to die by her side.
i don't let anyone know that when my father died
i watched his chest rise and fall, until his very last breath,
and then i screamed out in distress.
my family left me alone in the room with his shell,
and i sat by his bed for a moment thinking to my myself,
"oh my God, this must be hell."
and i still think it is because every single time i close my eyes to dream,
i'm greeted with my father's face
but for some reason he's always slipping away from me,
and even in my sleep i watch him die over and over and over again.

everyone is always so shocked with how well i handle death,
but it's only because i think a little piece inside of me is also dead.

DEATH AND HIS WINE

i've met death several times.
i know his face
i know his eyes.
he comes in about twice a week,
at a tavern i work at
near the crossroads.

there's not much here but drunk lost souls,
a piano man,
a guitarist and some
washed up goals.

i recognize him as soon as he opens the door-
i know he is death because his skin is moon chalk white,
i know he is death because his eyes are midnight blue.

people often say they're black but
i have seen death enough times
and gazed into those eyes
enough to know
that they are blue.
death likes you to think they're black,
because it is more terrifying.
 but they are blue.

death floats across the hardwood floors
but no one turns their head.
sometimes i think he's invisible,
sometimes i think i'm dead,
because how does no one notice that death has just entered the tavern?

how does no one feel the chill of his cloak that glides behind him,
carrying the prophecy of judgement day?
men get so drunk they cannot even see catastrophe and doom
enter through the door,
turning his fingers over one another as he walks.

death sits on a stool in front of me and meets my eyes.

his eyes are blue.
they're not black,
they're always blue.
his nose is pointed,
and his lips are thin.

he taps his fingers that are practically bone
on the table in a rhythm that sounds like sin
and i know what he wants.
i pour a glass of deep red wine and slide it over to him.

he smiles, revealing teeth i think he steals from babies,
before their parents put a dollar under their pillow.
he puts another year.
then takes the human pearl and sucks the innocence out of it.

he takes a sip and closes his eyes,
letting out a small sigh.
you'd think that being death he'd be filled with pleasure,
cutting red threads and stealing lives,
but death is just like any other man.
at the end of the day, he needs a drink-
death is much more stressed than we think.

he pulls the glass away and licks his lips, revealing his tongue.
i know he is death because his tongue is not stained water colour wine red
but instead, it is, as it always is,
the colour of blood.

death then orders a steak-
he likes it raw.
he chews it with his hands,
and let's the blood dribble down his chin
and onto his black pants.

when he is done death licks his fingers and wipes his face.
he drops two coins on the table,
and in a voice that rattle like bones in a cage says,
"one for your work, and another some time,"
then, just as he floated in, he floats out.

he stops at the door for a moment,

a surprising change in
                        pattern.

he turns his blue eyes to me and says,
"a piece of advice, i seldom do give,
do not drive tonight,
it's a beautiful night to live."

i didn't understand his riddle,
but i know enough of this world to know that
if death speaks to you
you ought to listen.

i walked home that night, down the highway,
over the crossroads.
i saw devils out of the corner of my eyes,
and men bury bones in the dirt,
but i ignored them and went on my way.

the next day
on the news i saw a young girl had died,
she was in a car accident.
the piano man from my tavern
had decided to drink and drive.

but it's so ironic
i can't help but laugh,
because i gave him wine,
death saved my life.

WHAT I'VE LEARNED

being human doesn't mean being perfect -
humans have been broken from the beginning.
being human is being broken
 and life is trying to put your
                    p i e c e s
 backtogether.

then, when you're finally whole, you die.
your death becomes a piece of someone else's life,
one they also have to put back into place.

and repeat.

ENDING

dear rosemary,
as i get older i find
that the world is
getting so much colder.

thank you to everyone i
forced to read my poems.
i really hope you did not
lie when you said that they
were good…

Made in the USA
Monee, IL
07 May 2021